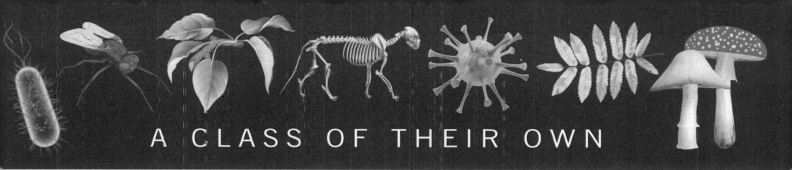

A CLASS OF THEIR OWN

Fungi

Mushrooms, Toadstools,
Molds, Yeasts, and Other Fungi

By
Judy Wearing

Crabtree Publishing Company
www.crabtreebooks.com

Crabtree Publishing Company

www.crabtreebooks.com

Author: Judy Wearing
Series consultant: Sally Morgan, MA, MSc, MIBiol
Project director: Ruth Owen
Designer: Alix Wood
Editors: Mark Sachner, Adrianna Morganelli
Proofreader: Crystal Sikkens
Project manager: Kathy Middleton
Print and production coordinator: Katherine Berti
Prepress technician: Katherine Berti

Developed & Created by Ruby Tuesday Books Ltd

Front cover: A chicken of the woods (*Laetiporus sulphureus*) fungus growing on a tree trunk. This is an edible wild mushroom.

Title page: A species of jelly fungus (*Ascocoryne sarcoides*)

Photographs:
George Barron, University of Guelph, CANADA: page 14
FLPA: front cover, pages 5 (bottom), 7 (all), 12, 15, 24, 27 (left), 28 (main), 33 (main), 34, 36 (top right), 36 (bottom center), 39, 40, 41, 43
Ruby Tuesday Books Ltd: pages 9 (top), 37, 42 (left)
www.savethefrogs.com: page 9 (bottom)
Science Photo Library: pages 5 (top), 6 (bottom), 8, 10, 11, 16, 17, 18, 21, 22, 23, 25, 26 (top), 29, 30 (right), 32, 35, 42 (right)
Shutterstock: pages 6 (top), 13 (left), 13 (right), 19 (bottom), 26 (bottom), 27 (right), 28 (top), 31 (top), 33 (inset), 36 (top center), 36 (bottom right), 38 (top), 38 (bottom)
USDA Forest Service: page 31 (bottom)
Wikipedia: pages 1, 19 (top), 30 (left), 36 (top left), 36 (bottom left)

Library and Archives Canada Cataloguing in Publication

Wearing, Judy
    Fungi : mushrooms, toadstools, molds, yeasts, and other fungi / Judy Wearing.

(A class of their own)
Includes index.
ISBN 978-0-7787-5375-9 (bound).--ISBN 978-0-7787-5389-6 (pbk.)

    1. Fungi--Classification--Juvenile literature.
2. Fungi--Juvenile literature. I. Title.
II. Series: Class of their own

QK603.2.W42 2010   j579.01'2   C2009-907432-X

Library of Congress Cataloging-in-Publication Data

Wearing, Judy.
    Fungi : mushrooms, toadstools, molds, yeasts, and other fungi / by Judy Wearing.
        p. cm. -- (A class of their own)
    Includes index.
    ISBN 978-0-7787-5389-6 (pbk. : alk. paper) -- ISBN 978-0-7787-5375-9 (reinforced library binding : alk. paper)
    1. Fungi--Juvenile literature. I. Title. II. Series.

    QK603.5.W43 2010
    579.5--dc22
                                    2009051343

Crabtree Publishing Company

www.crabtreebooks.com   1-800-387-7650
Copyright © **2010 CRABTREE PUBLISHING COMPANY.** All rights reserved. No part of this publication may be reproduced, stored in a retrieval system or be transmitted in any form or by any means, electronic, mechanical, photocopying, recording, or otherwise, without the prior written permission of Crabtree Publishing Company. In Canada: We acknowledge the financial support of the Government of Canada through the Canada Book Fund for our publishing activities.

Published in Canada
Crabtree Publishing
616 Welland Ave.
St. Catharines, Ontario
L2M 5V6

Published in the United States
Crabtree Publishing
347 Fifth Ave
Suite 1402-145
New York, NY 10016

Published in the United Kingdom
Crabtree Publishing
Maritime House
Basin Road North, Hove
BN41 1WR

Published in Australia
Crabtree Publishing
Unit 3 – 5 Currumbin Court
Capalaba
QLD 4157

Contents

WHAT ARE FUNGI?

Fungi are neither plants nor animals. Yet, like both groups, fungi are eukaryotic, which means that their cells have a membrane around the nucleus. In contrast, the cells of bacteria do not have such a membrane. These cells are prokaryotic. Some fungi have only one cell and so are unicellular. Most fungi have more than one cell and are thus multicellular.

Keeping Tabs on Fungi

There are about 98,000 known species of fungi, and 100 more species are discovered by scientists every month. No one knows for sure how many fungi species there are, but it ould be as many as 1.5 million. The scientists who study fungi are called mycologists.

CASE STUDY

Kingdom or Domain?

The way life-forms are grouped, or classified, is constantly changing. Traditionally, organisms were classified as either animal or plant. Over the years, many organisms have been grouped *alongside* animals and plants, rather than *within* those two groups. For years, the classification of living things has been based on six *kingdoms* of life—animals, plants, fungi, protists, bacteria, and archaea.

As scientists improve their understanding of the genetic makeup of living things, they can better compare organisms. This understanding has helped scientists figure out even more detailed groupings of living things. In the past, organisms were grouped according to their appearance. Appearances can be misleading, however. Two organisms may look similar, but their genetic makeup can be very different. For example, some yeasts might be taken for bacteria based on the fact that, like bacteria, they consist of a single round cell. Today, yeasts are known to be fungi, not bacteria.

Some scientists now believe that organisms should be classified using an even bigger grouping than kingdom. This level is called the *domain*. These scientists propose that life should be divided into three domains—Eukarya, Bacteria, and Archaea. Within the domain Eukarya are the four kingdoms of animals, plants, fungi, and protists. These kingdoms are more closely related to each other than to the domains of bacteria and archaea.

This is where things stand—for now. As scientists continue to make new discoveries, this system will undoubtedly turn out to be another chapter in the story of life!

They have plenty of work to keep them busy! Mycologists study fungi in the outdoors or wherever fungi grow, but they also study them in the laboratory. To do this, mycologists grow fungi in a nutrient-rich gel, in sterile dishes. These dishes, called petri dishes, have loose covers on them so the growing fungi's spores do not accidentally get mixed up or start to grow where they are unwanted.

Above: A scientist is growing different types of fungi during a study into parasitic fungi that can be used to kill the weeds and insect predators that attack crops. This is a natural alternative to using chemical pesticides.

Fungus growing on logs in Sumatra, Indonesia

Mushrooms and toadstools are the best-known fungi, but there are many other kinds. Bracket fungi, which look like shelves on tree trunks, are fungi, as are puffballs, the mold that grows on old bread and rotting fruit, and the brown spots on apples. Many fungi, such as the yeast that is used to make bread and pizza dough, are used to make food or to produce chemicals for industry and medicine. Some fungi cause disease, and some damage crops. Fungi are also important to us because they decompose dead plants and animals and provide plants with nutrients. Life on Earth relies heavily on fungi for its health.

A fresh apple and a decomposing apple covered with mold

The Classification of a Fungus

Classification within the fungi is changing as scientists continue to study DNA and improve their understanding of the genetic relationships of organisms. All fungi are members of the domain Eukarya and the kingdom Fungi. They are next organized into seven broad groups, called phyla. Mushrooms and toadstools are all in the phylum containing club fungi. Most other known fungi fall into two other phyla: those containing the pin molds and the sac fungi.

The common mushroom, also known as the button mushroom and the white mushroom, is a member of the phylum containing club fungi. Its scientific name, *Agaricus bisporus,* is made up of the names of its two most narrow groupings, genus and species.

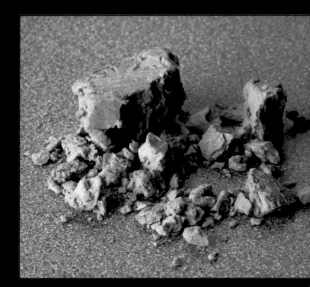

Baker's yeast

CLASSIFICATION OF THE BUTTON MUSHROOM		
Domain:	Eukarya	Organisms made up of complex cells
Kingdom:	Fungi	Fungi
Phylum:	Basidiomycota	The club fungi, includes bracket fungi, jelly fungi, smuts, and rusts
Class:	Agaricomycetes	Mushrooms
Order:	Agaricales	Fungi with spore-producing "gills"
Family:	Agaricaceae	Stalk usually bears a ring
Genus:	*Agaricus*	Caps that are not brightly colored
Species:	*Agaricus bisporus*	The button, or common, mushroom sold in grocery stores

The mushrooms on this farm are grown in large, sterile plastic sacks of compost.

THE GROCERY STORE MUSHROOM

Ninety percent of all mushrooms grown in Europe and North America for food are one species, Agaricus bisporus. The white button mushrooms on the shelves of grocery stores, the brown creminis, and the large portobello mushrooms are all of this same species. They grow naturally in meadows, where they feed on dead plant matter. On mushroom farms, they are grown on composted straw (straw that has been left to rot over a period of time with manure and fertilizer so it has begun to break down into soil).

CHAPTER ONE

THE BIOLOGY OF FUNGI

With nearly 100,000 known species and possibly more than a million more waiting to be discovered, fungi have great variety in body shape and structure. They do share some common features, however.

Threads and Fuzz: Hyphae and Mycelia

Most fungi grow as long, thin tubes called hyphae. Hyphae are too tiny to be seen without a microscope. Most fungi grow so many hyphae, however, that they form a mass that can be seen. This mass of hyphae is called a mycelium. An example of a mycelium is the round blob of fuzz formed by mold growing on a piece of old bread.

In some species, each hypha is one very long cell. In most species of fungi, however, a hypha is a chain of cells, each containing one or more nuclei. Rigid cell walls surround all hyphae, but hyphae are so small that most are delicate and easily broken.

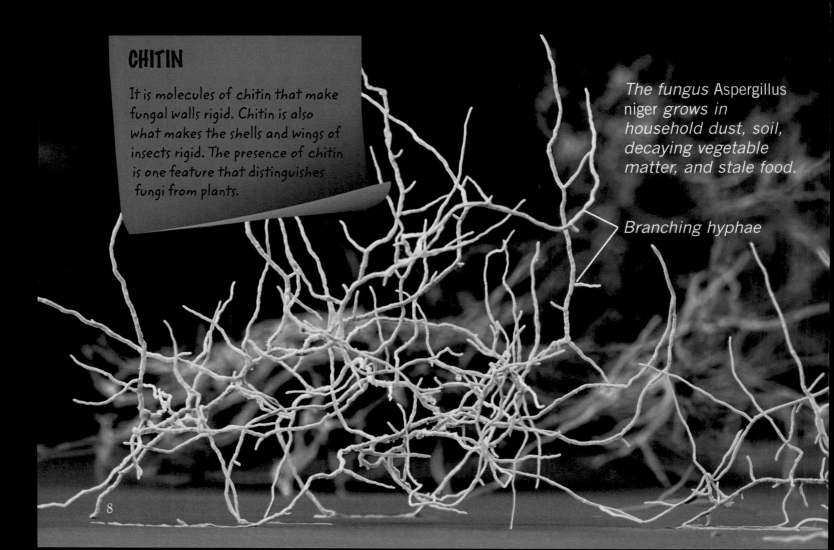

CHITIN

It is molecules of chitin that make fungal walls rigid. Chitin is also what makes the shells and wings of insects rigid. The presence of chitin is one feature that distinguishes fungi from plants.

The fungus Aspergillus niger *grows in household dust, soil, decaying vegetable matter, and stale food.*

Branching hyphae

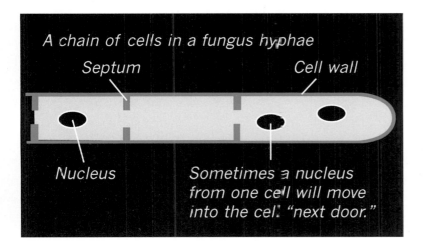

A chain of cells in a fungus hyphae

Septum

Cell wall

Nucleus

Sometimes a nucleus from one cell will move into the cell "next door."

Within hyphae, cross walls, called septa, separate cells into compartments. In some fungi, septa completely separate the cells from each other. In other fungi, septa only partially separate cells. In these fungi, hypha cells share their parts! The nucleus of one cell is able to travel through the opening in the septum into the cell "next door."

How Hyphae Grow

Hyphae grow from their tips. As long as the fungus has adequate food, water, and space, hyphae can keep on getting longer and longer.

Hyphae also grow in a branching pattern, like a tree. A new branch will start in a region on the side of a hypha where there are nutrients nearby. If there is a lot of extra food where a fungus is growing, its hyphae will grow many branches. The best-fed hyphae are the fuzziest.

Hyphae also grow out from the center of a fungus in every direction. This is why molds so often look round.

One-Cell Wonders: Unicellular Fungi

Some fungi do not exist as hyphae, but rather as single, round cells. Yeasts have this growth form, but they are not the only fungi to do so. Chytrids are a group of unicellular fungi, whose cells have long, thin hairs extending from them that look like roots. Chytrids are primitive fungi that represent a link between the group Fungi and the unicellular group Protista.

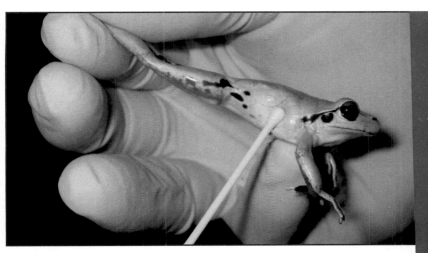

A scientist takes a skin swab from a frog to test for chytridiomycosis.

A KILLING FUNGUS

A species of chytrid is causing a disease in frogs and toads. Discovered in 1999, this disease, called chytridiomycosis, is spreading around the world. In areas where the fungus thrives, it has killed up to 80 percent of all frogs and toads within a single year. The disease kills the frogs by interfering with electrical charges in the frogs' bodies and causing a heart

Shape Changers: Dimorphic Fungi

Some fungi change their form. Sometimes they grow as hyphae, and sometimes they are a unicellular yeast. *Candida albicans* is one of these fungi, which are known as *dimorphic* because they exist in two forms. This fungus exists as a yeast in 80 percent of humans, where it lives in the intestines and does little harm. At other times, especially in people who are already weakened by an illness, this organism may grow hyphae. The hyphae growth of *Candida*, if it occurs in the blood, can cause people to become extremely ill. A *Candida* infection in the throat can be sore and itchy, but it is not life threatening.

How Fungi Reproduce

The different ways that fungi multiply are complex, but there are some common features. Most fungi can reproduce in two ways: asexually and sexually. With asexual reproduction, an individual fungus makes little copies of itself, like "clones." With sexual reproduction, the cells of two individuals come together and combine their DNA. Sexual reproduction is beneficial because some of the new mixtures of DNA will have a better chance of surviving.

In both sexual and asexual reproduction, most fungi reproduce by making spores, which are like fungi "seeds." Spores are microscopic packets containing the parts of a cell, including the nucleus, that are necessary to grow into a new individual. Because so few spores survive, fungi produce millions of them. Although we are not able to see them, fungal spores are everywhere around us—in the soil, in the air, and in the water.

Being tiny, spores are also light and travel easily. Spores are thus carried through the air and water to new places. This is how a fungus spreads.

Soya bean leaf

Rust fungus spores

A scanning electron microscope image of rust fungus spores on a soya bean leaf. The spores have formed inside a gall, an abnormal structure caused by the fungus, on the surface of the leaf. The spores are now erupting from the leaf and will go on to infect more plants.

Making Copies: Asexual Reproduction in Fungi

Most fungi make copies of themselves by asexually producing spores. In some species, the ends of hyphae become spore makers, which pinch off sections of cell wall, each containing material for a spore. In others, sporangia form in the hyphae. Sporangia are like "factories," making and releasing many spores. Sometimes they are round and sit on a hypha stalk. They can also grow as a cluster of stalks, as branches on a single stalk, or in the shape of a hollow container. Sporangia are often microscopic, but there are some species with sporangia that can be seen without a microscope.

SPORES: SURVIVING THROUGH THICK AND THIN

All spores have a cell wall. Some have a very thick wall, which allows them to survive poor conditions such as lack of water and hot or cold temperatures. These spores can survive for decades or even hundreds of years!

Other spores have a thin cell wall and cannot survive for long periods. As long as the conditions are good, however, these spores will grow quickly into a new fungus. A fungus growing in moist conditions with plenty of food is likely to produce this kind of spore.

A scanning electron microscope image of a bread mold sporangium

11

Mixing DNA: Sexual Reproduction in Fungi

The end result of sexual reproduction in fungi is always the formation of spores.

Individual fungi come together to mate and combine their DNA in several ways. In some species, a "mating spore" from one fungus combines with a hypha of another. In other species, two hyphae join together. In yet other species, there are particular mating parts with different shapes that must connect for DNA sharing to take place.

A mated fungus grows a structure to be the "spore factory" that makes and releases spores. These structures are called fruiting bodies. They are the largest structures of any fungi—and also the most recognizable. What we know as mushrooms and toadstools, morels, puffballs, and truffles are all fruiting bodies. Not all fruiting bodies produce the spores the same way. In mushrooms, the gills, which are on the underside of the cap, are the site of spore production and release. In puffballs, spores are produced inside and released into the air all at once, when the puffball explodes.

Not all fruiting bodies are mushrooms or truffles, and not all are large enough to see with the unaided eye. In fact, many fungi have microscopic fruiting bodies that produce even tinier spores.

A puffball mushroom explodes, sending a cloud of spores into the air.

Fungal Food: How Fungi Get Nutrients

Unlike plants, fungi cannot photosynthesize. That is, they cannot use energy from the Sun to make their own sugars for food. Instead, fungi are heterotrophs. This means that they get nutrients from "ready-made" matter in their environment in a wide variety of ways.

Nature's Clean-Up Crew: Saprotrophic Fungi

Most fungi feed on dead and decaying plants and animals. These fungi are saprotrophs. Along with bacteria, fungi are Earth's main decomposers. By feeding on dead and decaying matter, fungi keep the planet from piling up with dead things! If left long enough, a rotting vegetable will virtually disappear, completely consumed by fungi and bacteria.

In addition to freeing up space for other organisms to live and grow, fungi also recycle nutrients in dead cells for other organisms to use when they feed on fungi or on other living things that feed on fungi.

"Meat Eaters": Carnivorous Fungi

A few fungi are carnivores that actually catch tiny animals for food. There are 150 known species of carnivorous fungi, most of which live in soil. Tiny, common worms called nematodes are their favorite prey. Nematodes and other tiny organisms are caught in one of two ways:

• Special cells on the fungus's hyphae trap the nematode. In some species, the cells form a ring, and when a nematode enters the ring, the cells expand and then tighten around the nematode so it cannot escape. Hyphae then grow inside the dead nematode's body and digest it.

• Sticky juices are produced by the hyphae that trap prey when touched. When the struggling prey stops moving, hyphae grow into it and digest it.

Some mushrooms release their spores from their gills.

Gills

Gills

Arthrobotrys dactyloides: Nematode Killer

Arthrobotrys dactyloides lives in soil and grows as a long, slender network of hyphae. The fungus grows stalks that project out of the hyphae at periodic distances. Each stalk is made up of five long cells, end to end. The top three cells curl around to form a ring, though it might be more accurate to call it a noose. If a nematode puts its end into the lasso, the cells are triggered. In 0.1 second, the noose cells expand to three times their size, holding the nematode tight and trapping it. The trapped nematode thrashes violently, but it cannot escape. *Arthrobotrys dactyloides* then releases a toxin to speed up death. Its hyphae grow into the nematode's body, digesting it from the inside. Within four days, there will be no trace of the nematode left.

ARTHROBOTRYS DACTYLOIDES	
Kingdom:	Fungi
Phylum:	Ascomycota
Class:	Orbilomycetes
Order:	Orbiliales
Family:	Orbiliaceae
Genus:	*Arthrobotrys*
Species:	*Arthrobotrys dactyloides*

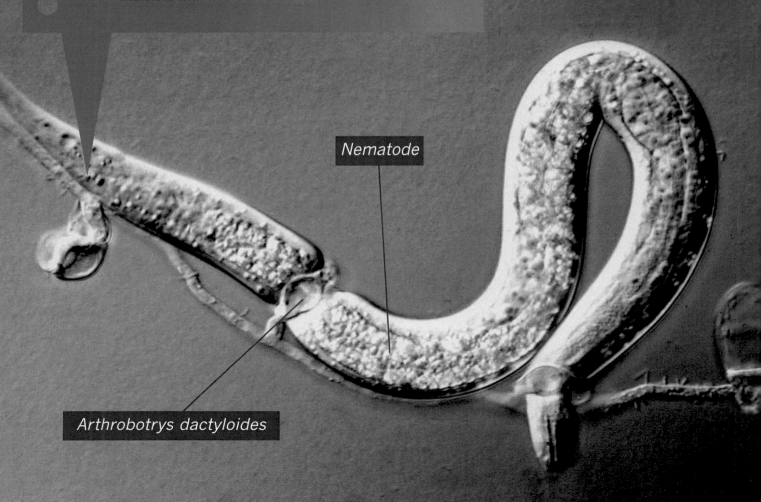

Nematode

Arthrobotrys dactyloides

Living with Others: Symbiotic Fungi

Some fungi are symbiotic, which means that they live closely with other species. In symbiotic relationships, one organism or both organisms may benefit from the relationship.

Fungi that live on plants and animals and feed on their nutrients or tissues are parasites. In this kind of symbiotic relationship, only one of the partners benefits—the parasite. Fewer fungi are parasites than decomposers, but parasitic fungi damage crops and cause disease, and so the parasites get a lot of attention.

Many fungi live in symbiotic relationships in which both organisms—the fungi and its host—benefit. This is called a mutualistic relationship.

Parasitic Fungi

Plant diseases caused by parasitic fungi have been closely studied. Dutch elm disease is one well-known example. Another is potato blight. The most notorious outbreak of potato blight was the Irish potato famine in the 1840s, during which one million people starved to death and another million were forced to leave Ireland to find other places to live.

Athlete's foot is caused by a fungus that lives on human skin. Fish and insects also play host to species of parasitic fungi. The white fuzz that is sometimes seen on the bodies of these creatures is the mycelium of a parasitic fungus. An animal with an infection like this is slowly being digested by its unwanted guest!

Mutualism: Depending on Fungi for Survival

Eighty to 90 percent of all plant species live mutualistically with fungi! Their partners are about six thousand species of soil fungi that live near, or in, their roots. Together, these fungi are known as mycorrhiza. Mycorrhiza benefit from their mutualistic relationship because their plant partners supply 10–35 percent of their food energy to their fungus, through its roots.

DUTCH ELM DISEASE

Dutch elm disease results when elm bark beetles bore tunnels into the wood and deposit a sac fungus that eats the wood. The tree reacts to the fungus invasion by plugging up its transport system for water and nutrients. The tree then withers and dies. Dutch elm disease was first noticed in Europe in 1910. It reached North America 20 years later and quickly spread. The disease is still attacking elm trees across the continent, and people are trying to stop it from getting into areas not yet affected. This photograph shows a of Dutch elm disease.

In return, the fungus supplies the plant with minerals such as nitrogen and potassium from the soil. Fungi are better at obtaining minerals than plants because hyphae can extend over a far larger area of soil than can roots. Mycorrhiza also provide plants with protection from disease. Plants grown in experiments without mycorrhiza are not as healthy as plants that are grown with mycorrhiza.

Members of the animal kingdom also benefit from this relationship. Without mycorrhiza, there would not be nearly as many plants in the world, and without plants to eat, there would not be nearly as many animals.

Lichen are another group of mutualistic fungi. They have a very close relationship with algae in which unicellular algae live inside the cells of the lichen. The algae produce food energy by photosynthesis and share it with the fungus. The fungus gets minerals from rock, soil, or wood and shares those minerals with the algae.

An Out-of-Body Experience: External Digestion

All fungi digest food outside their bodies! They do this by releasing through their hyphal walls enzymes that break down food. The small food molecules left over from digestion are then absorbed through the hyphal walls. Instead of "eating" their food, fungi grow in it.

Many fungi have an ability that most other organisms do not: they can digest substances such as cellulose, lignin, collagen, and keratin. These complex molecules are tough. They are what make wood and stems, connective tissue, and hair and nails tough. It is because fungi can break down these organic substances that they are so important as decomposers.

To digest such complex molecules, fungi need oxygen and water. Damp wood decays faster than dry wood because the fungi are better able to live and feed where it is wet.

The mycelium of this death cap fungus has a symbiotic relationship with beech trees, forming a mycorrhizal sheath around the roots of the tree.

The fungus Claviceps purpurea *has infected the grain shown here. When spread to humans, the disease caused by this fungus can bring about hallucinations, convulsions, and even death.*

CASE STUDY

Claviceps purpurea: Witchcraft or Bad Rye?

Claviceps purpurea is a fungus parasite of crops such as wheat and rye. It is found in most years, in most places, but usually in small amounts. The fungus infects the grain and causes a plant disease called ergot.

Ergot is more common in wet, cool weather. In these conditions, ergot can cause a lot of crop damage. Ergot is also poisonous to animals. Cows that are fed ergoty hay, or people who eat bread made from ergoty rye, can become very ill with ergotism. Ergotism causes hallucinations, vomiting, convulsions, and sometimes death. Ergotism was common in medieval times in Europe, when many people ate a lot of rye bread.

In 1693, several young girls in Salem, Massachusetts, were observed acting strangely and were accused, along with others, of being witches. The young girls were hallucinating, vomiting, and convulsing. Today, some people believe they were suffering from ergotism. Diaries of people from Salem show that the bread eaten that winter was made from rye grown in a very wet summer. This is one piece of evidence that supports the theory that the strange behavior in Salem was not caused by witchcraft but by a fungus.

CLAVICEPS PURPUREA

Kingdom: Fungi
Phylum: Ascomycota
Class: Sordariomycetes
Order: Hypocreales
Family: Clavicipitaceae
Genus: *Claviceps*
Species: *Claviceps purpurea*

CHAPTER TWO

THE PIN MOLDS

Pin molds represent about one percent of fungi species. Their common name comes from the appearance of the sporangia of some species. These sporangia take the form of tiny spheres on thin stalks, like pins in a pin cushion. Pin molds are also known as sugar molds, because they often grow on fruits with high sugar content, including strawberries.

Small and Fast-Growing Fungi

Pin molds are common in the soil and on rotting fruits and vegetables, but humans are often not aware of them because of their small size. Many pin molds are important decomposers, but some are parasites. A few species are parasites of other fungi! Only half of the pin molds have been grown in the laboratory, and most of these are in the group Mucorales, some of which are the fastest-growing fungi on the planet.

Pin molds have several features that distinguish them from other fungi. For one, the hyphae of most pin mold species do not have septa, or cross walls, while those of sac fungi and club fungi do. For these pin molds, the result is one-celled hyphae with many nuclei. For another, pin molds have a particular form of sexual reproduction. When conditions are right, specialized hyphae from two compatible individuals fuse. The result is the production of a single spore with DNA from both. This spore has thick walls and a highly ornamented surface with spikes, ridges, or both. The spore is called a zygospore, which has the same prefix as the scientific name for pin molds, Zygomycota. Though this means of sexual reproduction is unique, most pin molds reproduce asexually by producing multitudes of spores that are tiny copies of themselves.

A POTENTIAL THREAT

The pin mold common on damp bread also feeds on fruits such as bananas, grapes, and strawberries. Normally, it does not cause humans any problems, but for people with conditions that weaken their immune systems, it can cause a terrible disease, called zygomycosis. Though rare, zygomycosis is very dangerous. The pin mold fungi eat live tissues, killing cells in the process. Infection occurs most often on the face and inside the nose and can spread very quickly.

Sexual reproduction in a pin mold

Hypha

Zygospore

Distended tip of hypha

TEMPEH: A PIN MOLD DELICACY

At least 200 years ago, and maybe as long as 1,000 years ago, the people of Indonesia began adding pin mold to soybeans and eating the product. Called tempe, or tempeh, this food is made by mashing whole soybeans and adding spores of the pin mold *Rhizopus oligosporus*. The mixture is packed in plastic bags or banana leaves (as shown at right) and kept warm for 24 to 48 hours. During this time, the fast-growing mold creates a network of mycelia surrounding the soybeans, binding them together in a block. The tempeh is then cooked once good meat substitute. It has comp similar to meat, nuts, and mush

Blocks of processed tempeh
for sale in a market

*Pin molds growing
on a strawberry*

19

White Flies and Black Bread

Entomophthorales: a long name for a group of pin molds that means "insect destroyer" in Greek. (*Entomo* = insect; *phthor* = destroyer). As their name suggests, many Entomophthorales are parasites of insects, particularly flies. Flies infected with the "insect destroyer" fly up to as high a place as they can and glue themselves with their mouth to the surface. This behavior is caused by the parasite. The flies die in this position—stuck to glass, pine needles, or whatever is nearby. A white circle can be seen around the carcass of the fly. The circle is formed by a large number of tiny spores that have filled the fly's body in such quantity that the victim has burst open. The spores get sprayed in the process.

Other groups of pin molds are common on bread and moist grains. Like most pin molds, black bread mold mainly reproduces asexually. Tiny black sporangia grow on the surface of bread, which are visible as black specks among a white nest of hyphae. It is the color of the sporangia that give this mold its name. When the sporangia mature, they burst and release hundreds of spores into the air.

Pilobolus kleinii:
A Dung Fungus Squirt Gun

CASE STUDY

Pilobolus kleinii lives on cow and horse dung. Like other pin molds, its sporangia appear as tiny black spheres on thin, clear stalks. *Pilobolus kleinii* sporangia are different from those of other pin molds, however. As its common name—squirt gun fungus—suggests, each one is like a miniature squirt gun. The stalk is swollen with liquid under pressure. When the sporangium matures, the pressure in the stalk gets so high that the top of it explodes— and the black sporangium is shot up and away on a stream of water, just like a squirt gun.

When it "squirts," the *Pilobolus kleinii* sporangium is one of the fastest-moving natural objects in the air. The flying sporangium reaches speeds of up to 45 miles per hour (72 kilometers per hour). The power of the blast can shoot the sporangium nearly 10 feet (three meters) away.

The squirt gun fungus benefits the fungus by getting its spores onto blades of grass, where they can be eaten by cows. The spores pass through the cow and are deposited with its dung in a fresh pile of food. Just one to two days later, more squirt gun sporangia will form.

The Pilobolus *pin molds shown here display hyphae and sporangia that are similar to those that shoot* Pilobolus kleinii *sporangia into the air.*

PILOBOLUS KLEINII

Kingdom:	Fungi
Phylum:	Zygomycota
Class:	Zygomycetes
Order:	Mucorales
Family:	Philobolaceae
Genus:	*Pilobolus*
Species:	*Pilobolus kleinii*

Spores are released from these sac-like containers called sporangia.

Hypha

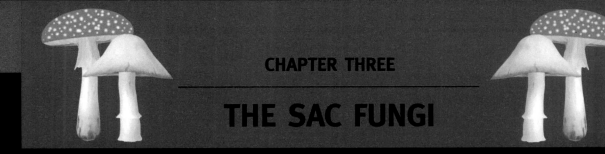

CHAPTER THREE

THE SAC FUNGI

Seventy-five percent of all known fungi are sac fungi, which so far adds up to about 30,000 known species. The group includes yeast and mycelial forms; many saprotrophs; mycorrhiza, lichens, and other symbionts; some parasites that cause important plant diseases; and a few predatory species.

Major Fungi

Sac fungi are found on land and in water, on all continents, and they include many of the most important fungi to human life. The species of yeast used to make bread, beer, and wine is a sac fungus, as are most yeasts. The fungus that produces the medicine penicillin also belongs to this group, as do the fungi that infect and kill chestnut and elm trees and the fungus that puts the "blue" in blue cheese. Many of these fungi are very well studied because of their importance to human commerce and health.

Sac fungi reproduce asexually and sexually. The particular ways sac fungi accomplish this distinguish them from other fungi groups.

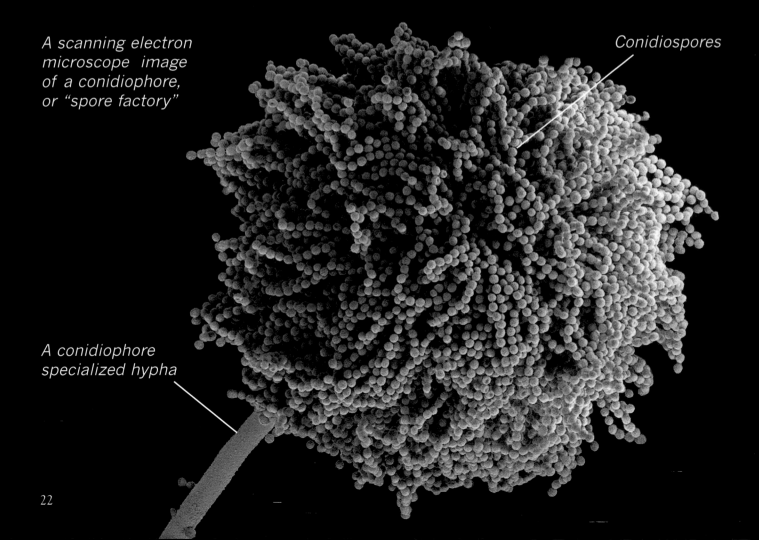

A scanning electron microscope image of a conidiophore, or "spore factory"

Conidiospores

A conidiophore specialized hypha

Asexual Reproduction

Yeasts, which are unicellular, reproduce asexually by first growing bigger and making a second nucleus. Then, a cell wall is produced down the middle, dividing the contents of the cell in two. This creates two daughter cells.

Yeasts also reproduce asexually by a process known as budding. First, a second nucleus develops within the cell. This second nucleus is "packaged" with any cell material it needs to form a complete fungus. Then, the new material is pushed out the cell wall, in a bud. The bud breaks off from the parent cell, leaving a scar in the cell wall where it exited.

Asexual reproduction in mycelial forms is accomplished via spores. The spores are produced at the ends of specialized hyphae, called conidiophores, which are the "spore factories." The spores released into the environment are called conidiospores or conidia.

Sexual Reproduction

Sexual reproduction occurs in numerous ways among sac fungi. The first step is for the DNA from two separate individuals to be combined during mating. In sac fungi yeast, two unicellular individuals join together to form one cell, doubling the size and doubling the DNA. In mycelial sac fungi, two hyphae join together, and nuclei from one are put into the other.

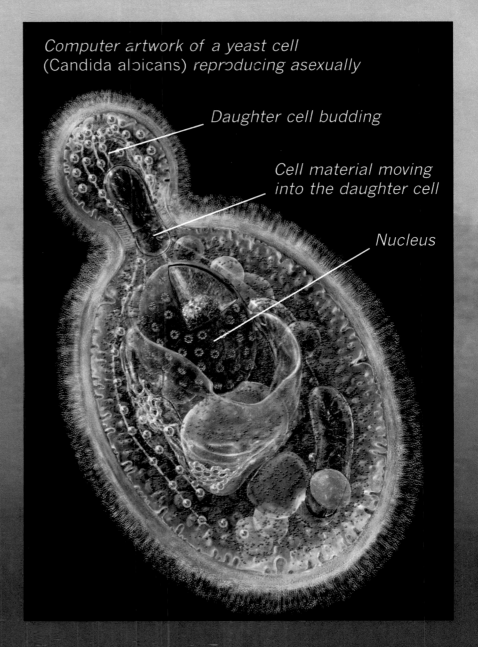

Computer artwork of a yeast cell (Candida albicans) reproducing asexually

Daughter cell budding

Cell material moving into the daughter cell

Nucleus

Putting the "Sac" in Sac Fungi

For all sac fungi, the result of sexual reproduction is a sac containing eight spores. The sac is called an ascus, which means "wineskin" in Greek—a reference to the shape of the sac. The spores it contains are called ascospores. The ascus gives this group of fungi its common name, the sac fungi, as well as its scientific name, Ascomycota.

Mated yeast cells form one ascus, which contains the eight ascospores that are released from it. In most other sac fungi, however, many asci are formed, perhaps even millions of them. In many species, the mated hyphae form a fruiting body, called an ascocarp. These fruiting bodies can be very large.

ASCOCARPS

Ascocarps take many forms, some of which are spectacular. Many are like mushrooms in that they have a wide structure on top of a stalk. Some of these structures have a shape similar to that of an umbrella, but many are shaped like cups, balls, or cylinders. They occur in a range of colors and textures. The largest ascocarp has a 40-inch (102-centimeter) high stalk with a 20-inch (51-cm) diameter cup on top. It is brown and looks like a thin, round plate delicately turned up at the edges.

Sac Fungi Yeast: Bread and Beer

Several sac fungi are important in the production of foods humans have consumed for thousands of years. One species in particular, *Saccharomyces cerevisiae,* has had a particularly large impact. This unicellular yeast is what makes bread, donuts, and pizza dough rise. This very same species is also used to make alcoholic beverages such as wine, beer, and whiskey. This explains its scientific name, which means "the sugar fungus of the beer."

Scarlet elf cap fungi

Brewer's Yeast

This yeast feeds on sugar. When it is added to grape juice and left in conditions without oxygen, it consumes sugars in the juice as food and produces alcohol in the process. The result is wine. The same thing happens when this yeast is added to a mixture of boiled grain, such as barley, put in bottles or casks where there is no oxygen. In these instances, the result is not wine, but beer. Humans have been making wine for at least 8,000 years, and many types of *Saccharomyces cerevisiae* have been produced. Each one is a little bit different, but all are the same species, and all are known as "brewer's yeast."

Baker's Yeast

When *Saccharomyces cerevisiae* feeds on sugar in the absence of oxygen, not only alcohol is produced, but also carbon dioxide. If this yeast is added to a mixture of flour and water, the yeast feeds on the sugars and produces carbon dioxide gas, making bubbles in the dough. The alcohol produced evaporates out of the dough and into the air when the dough is cooked. *Saccharomyces cerevisiae* is what makes bread rise, as well as pizza dough and donuts. When it is used to make these foods, it is known as "baker's yeast." Yeast was used to make bread rise at least 3,000 years ago, in ancient Egypt.

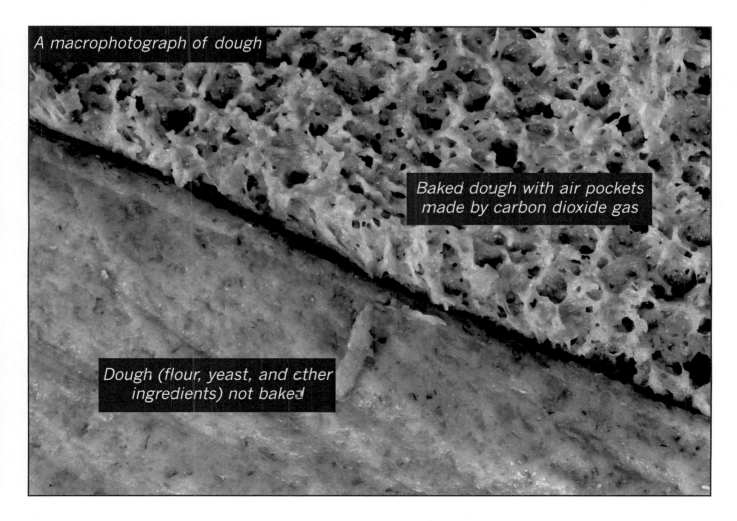

A macrophotograph of dough

Baked dough with air pockets made by carbon dioxide gas

Dough (flour, yeast, and other ingredients) not baked

Blue Spores, Blue Cheese

The threads of blue-green that wind through blue cheeses, such as Roquefort, Danish blue, Gorgonzola, and blue Stilton, are not cheese, but the asexual spores of *Penicillium roqueforti.* This sac fungus is named after the Roquefort cheese made in the French village of Roquefort. To make blue cheese, spores of this fungus are added to the cheese with the milk. Later, when the cheese is a solid block, holes are poked through it. The holes allow air to reach the insides of the cheese, allowing hyphae to grow. Over a period of a few weeks, hyphae cover the interior surfaces of tunnels and cracks and produce the blue-green spores that give the cheese its name and the strong, sharp flavor that is well loved by many.

Other cheeses are made with different fungi species. Brie and Camembert are two French cheeses with a white coating that surrounds a soft interior. The white coating is the mycelium of *Penicillium camemberti.*

A scanning electron microscope image of a blue vein in a piece of Stilton cheese

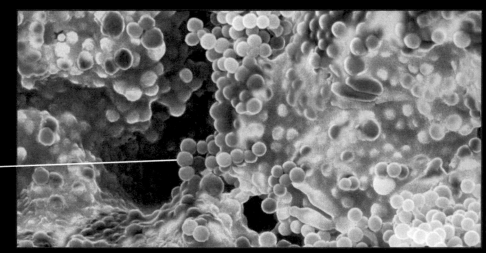

The blue beads are the spores of the fungus Penicillium roqueforti *that give the cheese its flavor and color.*

Stilton cheese and crackers

Edible Ascocarps: Fruiting Bodies as Food

Some species of sac fungi are eaten directly. In fact, truffles, the fruiting bodies of some mycorhizzal sac fungi, are a delicacy around the world. Truffles are bulbous formations that form close to tree roots. Not all truffles are edible. Those that we can eat are hunted by dogs or pigs, which locate them by smell.

Morels are also fruiting bodies of mycorhizzal sac fungi. Morels are a little like mushrooms in that they are rounded bodies that grow above ground on stalks. They look very different from mushrooms, however, in that they have a deeply wrinkled, honeycomb appearance all over. Morels appear in spring, and many are delicious. Some have mild flavor, but others have a strong, nutty taste. Other morel-like ascocarps are poisonous, so people must take care to know which species are edible and which are not.

DON'T MESS WITH FAKE MORELS

A group of poisonous ascocarps, known as "false morels," look similar to morels, but their wrinkles do not look like honeycomb. Instead the pattern of the wrinkles is more irregular, like the wrinkles of the brain (as shown above). Some people risk eating false morels despite the poison. They think that by boiling them in water, often twice, they may be able to get rid of the poison. The poison is so potent, however, that a person who stands near the boiling water and breathes in the toxin could become ill.

FERMENTED SOY JUICE

Another sac fungus that has been helping humans produce food for thousands of years is Aspergillus oryzae, a key element in the making of soy sauce. Traditional Japanese soy sauce is made by fermenting cooked soybeans with wheat and Aspergillus oryzae, then adding water and salt and aging it for six months. Aspergillus oryzae is also used to make miso—a flavorfu paste of fermented beans famous as the key ingredient in miso soup. Sake, Japanese rice wine is made with Aspergillus oryzae.

Italy's Fungal Treasure

Between August and December each year, in the region of Piedmont in northern Italy, men and dogs take to the woods. They are searching for the white Piedmont truffle, a rare species that does not grow anywhere else in the world. The truffle—the fruiting body of the mycorrhiza *Tuber magnatum*—is found associated with the roots of oak, willow, poplar, and linden trees. The dogs sniff them out and show their masters where to dig. Digging is done gently to avoid damaging the hyphae and tree roots, so there will be more truffles the following year.

The collected truffles are carefully cleaned with a brush and stored in a cool place. Because they are rare and considered delicious by many, the truffles are worth a lot of money. One-quarter pound (113.4 grams) can cost more than $500 U.S. The truffles are eaten raw and in slices on pasta, meat, and egg dishes.

TUBER MAGNATUM

Kingdom:	Fungi
Phylum:	Ascomycota
Class:	Pezizomycetes
Order:	Pezizales
Family:	Tuberceae
Genus:	*Tuber*
Species:	*Tuber magnatum*

Wonder Drugs

Prior to the days when antibiotics were discovered, a chest infection or a cut on a finger could result in death. Antibiotics are drugs that kill bacteria. The first antibiotic in history was penicillin, which was discovered purely by accident in 1928 by the scientist Alexander Fleming. He noticed a mold growing in his experiments that killed the bacteria around it. He identified the mold as the sac fungus *Penicillium notatum*. It wasn't until the 1940s that researchers figured out how to grow Penicillium in large quantities to produce penicillin and use it to fight infection in humans.

Today, the chemistry of antibiotics is well understood. Many other antibiotic chemicals have been found in nature, some of them produced by fungi. Scientists have also figured out how to produce some antibiotics from scratch.

MORE MEDICINES: INSULIN

In addition to antibiotics, sac fungi are used to produce proteins, such as insulin. Insulin is a protein made by the body that is critical for converting sugar to energy. Diabetes is the name of the disease some people have in which their body does not produce enough insulin. Sac fungi are used to produce insulin in laboratories for diabetic people to use. To do this, the human gene that directs a cell to make insulin is put into the gene of the sac fungus. The gene instructs the fungus cells to make human insulin.

LOOKING OUT FOR NUMBER ONE

There are several fungi that produce penicillin. While penicillin is of great benefit to us, that is not why the fungus produces it. The fungus produces it because it is of benefit to itself! Penicillin benefits the fungus by killing bacteria around it. Fewer organisms growing around the fungus results in less competition for food. This means more food for the fungus.

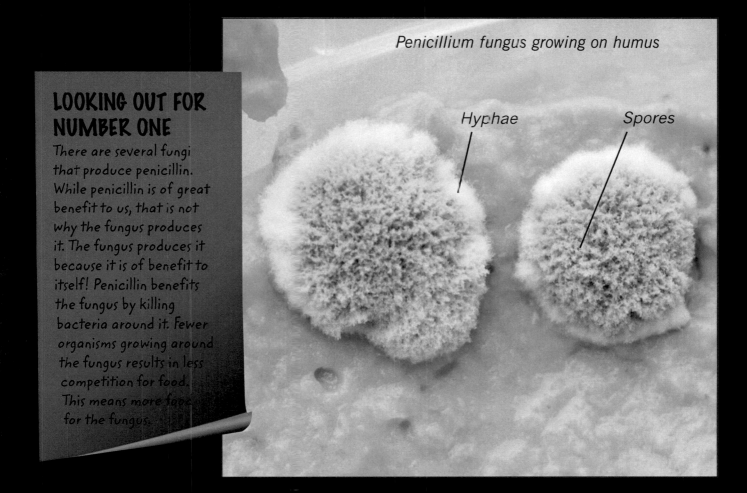

Penicillium fungus growing on humus

Hyphae

Spores

Technology Tools

Fungi are relatively easy to grow, and they produce a number of interesting proteins and chemicals all on their own. This has led to various uses in technology, and today, fungi assist in the production of an increasing number of chemicals.

Back in the 1920s, citric acid was produced from Italian lemons. Today, *Aspergillus niger* is cultured, or grown, to be used to produce citric acid. This chemical, which is found naturally in lemons and other citrus fruits, makes these foods taste tart. It is added to soft drinks, juices, and other foods to give them that tart taste. Citric acid has other uses, too, in water softeners and detergents and as a cleaner. To produce citric acid without the citrus fruit, big vats of the fungus are fed sugar from inexpensive sources such as corn syrup and molasses. As part of its metabolism, the fungus makes citric acid.

Comfortable Clothing

Sac fungi are also used to make clothing and textiles. For example, the stone-washed look for jeans can be created using a group of sac fungi, called *Trichoderma*, that break down cellulose in the denim cloth, giving it a white look and soft feel. The same species are being used in a process called biopolishing. Fibers such as cotton and linen, which come from plants and thus

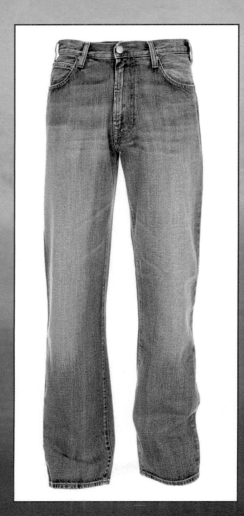

have cellulose, can be fuzzy and create a coarse feel to the cloth. *Trichoderma* is added to the cloth, and it eats the cellulose fuzz, leaving the cloth smooth and soft. Still other sac fungi species produce enzymes that break down dyes used to color textiles. The fungi, which remove color and destroy toxins, are being used to help clean waste water from textile factories.

A culture of the fungus Trichoderma *used for fading denim cloth*

Dreadful Diseases in Plants

Many diseases of plants and animals including humans, are the result of infection by sac fungi. A few of these are particularly famous, chestnut blight among them. This condition—and the fungus that causes it—was first discovered on American chestnut trees in 1904 in the Bronx Zoo in New York City. By 1930, 50 percent of all chestnut trees in North America were infected and dying. Today, the American chestnut is a threatened species.

The fungus that did this damage came from Asia, where it grows on a different species of chestnut tree, the Chinese chestnut. The fungus harms the Chinese chestnut but does not kill it. Unfortunately, American chestnut trees are more susceptible to the disease. On American chestnut, the fungus appears as an orange area on the bark where it is actively producing spores. The fungus spreads, killing the bark as it does so. Eventually, the bark is destroyed in a strip that reaches right around the tree's trunk. This cuts off the transportation of water and nutrients, and the tree dies.

The fungus Taphrina deformans *causes the disease called leaf curl.*

There are many more examples of sac fungi diseases. Leaf curl affects peaches; corn leaf blight affects corn; powdery mildew affects clover, beans, soybeans, and grapes; and brown rot affects peaches and cherries. Ergot, the disease of grains such as rye and wheat, which causes ergotism in animals, is also due to sac fungi.

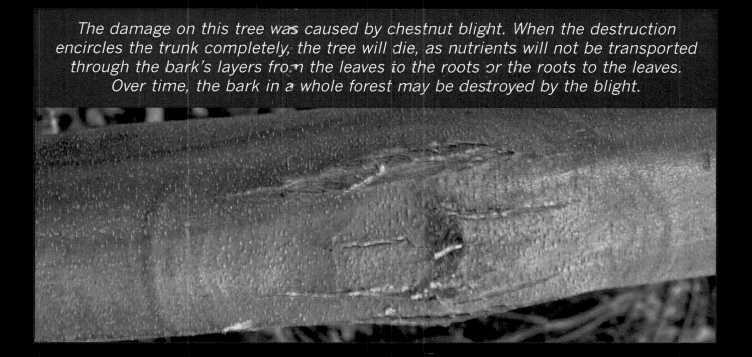

The damage on this tree was caused by chestnut blight. When the destruction encircles the trunk completely, the tree will die, as nutrients will not be transported through the bark's layers from the leaves to the roots or the roots to the leaves. Over time, the bark in a whole forest may be destroyed by the blight.

Terrible Toxins

Sac fungi include many of the most useful species in the Fungi kingdom. They also include some of the most dangerous. In chapter one, we read about *Candida albicans*, the yeast that lives in the guts of humans and mammals and can cause disease in people whose immune systems are not working well. Serious infection can result if the yeast gets into the bloodstream, but this is unlikely to happen in healthy individuals.

Close relatives of the fungus that is used to make soy sauce, *Aspergillus flavus* and *Aspergillus parasiticus*, both produce aflatoxins, which are among the worst toxins known. Even a small amount of aflatoxin can seriously harm livestock and people alike. The molds that produce it grow on nuts and grains all over the world, especially in warm, moist climates. When animals and humans eat food from infected plants, they can become very ill.

An animal that ingests a large amount of aflatoxin at once can die. The toxin causes liver failure and breaks down blood cells. In people, the limbs can swell with water, and stomach cramps are common. Smaller amounts of aflatoxin over a longer period of time can result in cancer, liver disease, and a malfunctioning immune system.

In the United States, $100 million worth of crops are destroyed every year due to *Aspergillus* infection. When food shortages occur in countries such as India and China, cases of human poisonings happen all too often.

Athlete's foot and ringworm are infections of a species of fungus that lives on skin, making the area sore and itchy.

A colored scanning electron microscope image of athlete's foot fungus hyphae

Skin flakes (blue)

Marvelous Mutualists: Lichens and Algae

Some sac fungi are mycorrhiza, which means that they live underground in and among roots. These fungi have mutualistic relationships with the plants around them, providing the plant with minerals from the soil as the plants provide the fungus with carbohydrates for energy. Some of these sac fungi, such as truffles and morels, are mycorrhiza of trees. They are, however, a small fraction of the total number of fungi species that form this type of mycorrhiza.

Sac fungi have another important mutualism: lichens. Lichens are fungi that have algae living in them. Some scientists describe lichens as "farmers" that grow algae in their cells to provide food. While lichens rely on the algae to provide them with carbohydrates and could not survive without them, some algae survive just fine outside of their fungi, if given the chance. With the help of their algae, lichens can live on bare rock. They produce chemicals that break the rock down, and then they absorb the minerals and share them with their algae partners. Rocks are not particularly nutritious, and algae supply their fungus partner not only with energy but also with vitamins. The lichens also provide water to the algae for photosynthesis, and they protect algae from the Sun's harmful UV (ultraviolet) rays.

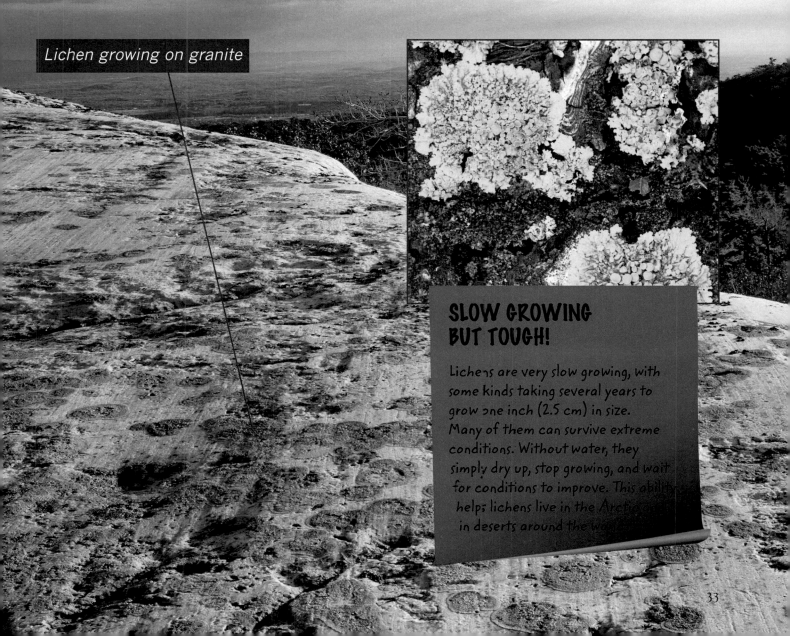

Lichen growing on granite

SLOW GROWING BUT TOUGH!

Lichens are very slow growing, with some kinds taking several years to grow one inch (2.5 cm) in size. Many of them can survive extreme conditions. Without water, they simply dry up, stop growing, and wait for conditions to improve. This ability helps lichens live in the Arctic or in deserts around the world.

Tough to Pin Down

There have been about 15,000 different lichens described, about 13,500 of them sac fungi. Classifying lichens is tricky, because they are not one species. They are made up of two, and in some cases even three, species. Lichens have many forms and colors. Some, such as reindeer moss, look leafy and grow several inches tall. Others look more like splashes of paint on the surface of rocks or trees. Lichens range in color from white to black, with red, orange, and yellow species, too.

More Marvelous Mutualists: Fungi and Animals

A few sac fungi have mutualist relationships with animals. For example, a species of snail that lives in salt marshes nibbles on marsh grass and deposits fungal spores on the ground. It comes back later to feed on the growing fungus it "planted." Other sac fungi are mutualists with bark and ambrosia beetles. Each spring, female beetles chew a tunnel into trees and deposit fungal spores they've carried with them. The fungus grows in the cavity, feeding on wood. The beetles lay eggs in the tunnels, and the young feed on the fungus. Many other beetles that feed on wood have unicellular sac fungi in their guts. The fungi help them digest their food. In these situations, beetles and fungi both greatly benefit from the relationship. The tree, however, does not.

Striped ambrosia beetle adult, pupa, and larva are shown from left to right in the bark of a Douglas fir tree.

The larvae of the beetles feed on the fungus seen blackening the tree's bark at the bottom of the photograph.

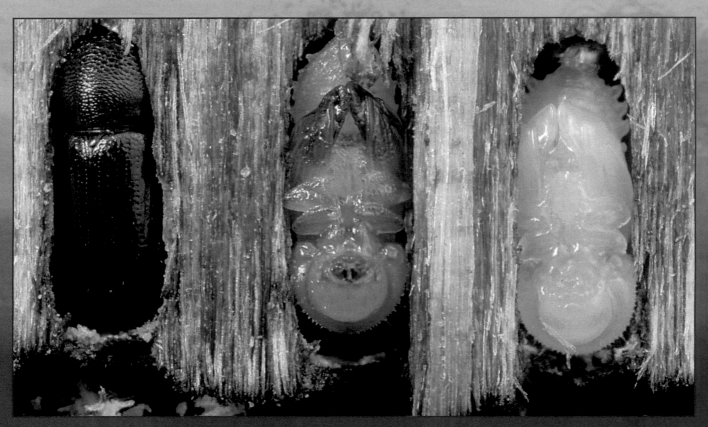

From Vacation to Organ Transplants

CASE STUDY

When Jean-Francois Borel was on vacation in Norway in 1969, he collected samples of fungi from the soil and brought them home to Switzerland. In his laboratory, he tested the samples, looking for new antibiotics. One of the samples, *Tolypocladium inflatum*, produced a chemical he named cyclosporine. Cyclosporine turned out to not be useful as an antibiotic, but Borel noticed it had another property—it decreased the immune system and prevented white blood cells from attacking foreign cells.

This might sound like a bad thing, but Borel recognized that cyclosporine could be very useful for organ transplant patients. When an organ from one body is put into another, the patient's immune system recognizes the cells as foreign to the body and attacks them. For organ transplants to work, the patient's own immune system has to be stopped from destroying the new organ. Before cyclosporine, the only drugs available to do this prevented all components of the immune system from working, and many transplant patients died from pneumonia and other infections. Their bodies could not fight illness. Since 1983, organ transplant patients are given cyclosporine, which more selectively targets parts of the immune system, greatly improving the chances of survival.

TOLYPOCLADIUM INFLATUM

Kingdom:	Fungi
Phylum:	Ascomycota
Class:	Sordariomycetes
Order:	Hypocreales
Family:	Ophiocordycipitaceae
Genus:	*Tolypocladium*
Species:	*Tolypocladium inflatum*

This scanning electron microscope image shows a white blood cell engulfing and digesting bacteria (red) inside a human body. The fungus Tolypocladium inflatum *reduces the ability of white blood cells to attack foreign cells. This increases the chances that our bodies will accept the presence of transplanted organs without attacking and rejecting them.*

CHAPTER FOUR

CLUB FUNGI

All of the toadstools and mushrooms in the world belong to one group of fungi—Basidiomycota, the club fungi. There are about 30,000 known species of club fungi, which is about one-third of all described fungi species in the world.

Worldwide Fungi

Club fungi vary greatly in appearance and structure—perhaps more than in any other fungi group. Toadstools and mushrooms are the fruiting bodies of some species, whose mycelia, or network of hyphae, extend underground in mats that we cannot see. These species are either saprotrophs feeding on wood or mycorrhiza associated with trees and other plants. Bracket fungi and puffballs are also club fungi, and there are some yeasts, too. There are also a few lichens in this group, and other mutualists, as well as parasites of plants and animals. Club fungi occur on land and in water, in habitats all over the world. Several common varieties are shown below.

Jack-o-lantern fungus   Spiny puffball   Bracket fungus

Chicken of the woods fungus   Scarlet waxcap   Shiitake mushrooms

Reproduction in Club Fungi: More Sexual Than Asexual

Like other fungi, club fungi reproduce asexually and sexually, though asexual reproduction is much less common in club fungi than in other groups. Asexual reproduction occurs most regularly in the club fungi yeasts. These yeasts reproduce asexually by budding, just as yeasts in other groups do. In some species, asexual spores are made in specialized hyphae called conidiophores, and the spores they make are called conidiospores.

A few mycelial species of club fungi are only known to reproduce asexually. No fruiting bodies have ever been observed, but it is quite possible that sexual reproduction occurs and that scientists have simply not seen it yet.

Sexual Reproduction

In sexual reproduction in club fungi, the hyphae of two individuals mate, transferring DNA material from one to the other, so that one of the hyphae has double the DNA. This mated fungus continues to grow, until the hyphae form a structure, or fruiting body, called a basidiocarp . Puffballs, mushrooms, and brackets are all kinds of basidiocarps.

Cells within the basidiocarp form club-shaped "spore factories" called basidia. These are equivalent to the ascus produced by sac fungi and give the group of club fungi its scientific name, Basidiomycota. The basidia of club fungi, in turn, produce spores called basidiospores. Basidiospores are made on the outside of the basidia, not on the inside. From there, they are released into the air for dispersal. When they land in a favorable place, basidiospores begin to grow into new fungi.

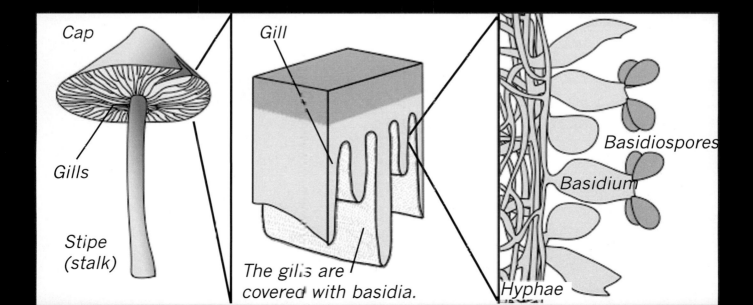

Cap

Gills

Stipe
(stalk)

Gill

The gills are
covered with basidia.

Basidiospores

Basidium

Hyphae

Umbrellas, Bird's Nests, and Jellies: Basidiocarp Diversity

Mushrooms look like a stalk with an umbrella-like top. Underneath the "umbrella" are gills, which appear as thin, flat segments, arranged in parallel. The surfaces of gills are covered with microscopic basidia, each one making spores at its end.

Other basidiocarps have a completely different appearance. Puffballs are spherical, with a papery thin shell. The basidia are contained inside. When rain drops on a mature puffball, the shell is broken and a cloud of basidiospores whooshes out into the air.

As their name suggests, bird's nest fungi look like several round balls inside a nest. The "eggs" are bundles of basidia, encased in a thick wall. When raindrops land inside the cup at a certain angle, an "egg" will be shot out of the nest onto the ground or into a tree, where the basidiospores are released.

Jelly fungi appear as blobs on tree branches or fallen logs. They are often bright colors. These basidiocarps are like jelly when there is a lot of moisture, but they shrivel up when it is dry. They are able to puff back up when they get wet again.

Bird's nest fungus

The "eggs" are filled with basidia.

Jelly fungus is growing on the branch of an oak tree.

Fairy Rings

In meadows and lawns, a ring sometimes can be seen of darker green grass that is growing longer then the rest. After rain during the warm months, another ring appears. This ring consists of brown mushrooms along the outside of the dark grass. Such mushroom rings are known as fairy rings, and they were once thought to be the site of secret fairy dances.

In actual fact, the rings are caused by the growth pattern of a club fungus underground. The fungus' mycelium expands in a circle feeding on dead plant matter around the edge of the ring. The long green ring of grass indicates where hyphae from recent years have died, releasing nitrogen into the soil, which has fertilized the grass. The active growing hyphae are just beyond this circle. It is here that fruiting bodies are produced. Each year, the ring gets a little bigger as the fungus continues to grow outward. Some individual fairy fungi can live hundreds of years, giving the rings a chance to become quite large in the process. One fairy ring in France is over a half a mile (0.8 km) in diameter.

Wooly milkcap fungus in a fairy ring

Fungus Farms

In the jungles throughout South America and as far north as the forests of the northeastern United States, ants are busy farming. Large colonies send out thousands of workers, each of which cuts a semicircle of leaf to carry back to the nest. These leaf-cutter ants enter the nest's underground passages and pass their leaf pieces on to leaf processors, who remove unwanted matter from the leaf and smear fungal spores onto the leaf edge.

The pieces of leaves are kept in football-shaped gardens, where a species of fungus feeds on them. The ants, in turn, feed on the mycelium of the fungus. They also feed their larvae with it. This is a mutualistic relationship: the ants feed the fungus, and they also keep other fungi from invading the garden. They keep the garden clean and remove any debris. In this way, the fungi are provided with a good habitat and food.

Other club fungi are mutualists with bark beetles. Adult bark beetles bore holes into trees and leave fungal spores behind. The fungus grows, feeding on the wood. The beetle lays eggs in the wood, and the larvae that hatch from the beetle eggs feed on the fungus.

TERMITE FUNGUS FARMERS

A group of African termites farms club fungi in the same way as leaf-cutter ants do. The termites eat wood, then excrete the partially digested remains of their meals in their nest. Club fungi feed on the termite waste, and the termites feed on the fungi. The enzymes the fungi produce to break down cellulose in the wood remain active inside the guts of the termites and help them digest the wood they eat.

Leaf-cutter ants at work in their fungus farm.

Plant and People Parasites

Two groups of club fungi infect and cause damage to plants: rusts and smuts.

Rust fungi appear as rust-colored or yellow spots on stems and leaves. Under certain conditions, some of these fungi can completely ruin crops. Some rust fungi attack wheat and other grains, and others attack sugarcane, cotton, some vegetables, some flowers, coffee, and pine trees. Rust fungi destroy about 10 percent of the world's grain crops each year.

Smut fungi are another group of club fungi that attack plants. Most smut fungi, in contrast to the rusts, attack the kernels of grains and grasses. A few, however, do attack a plant's stems or leaves—or the plant's seeds before they emerge from the ground. Infected grain kernels are filled with black powder, which are the fungal spores. In addition to grains, plants such as sugarcane, carnations, rice, and onions have smut parasites.

Corn smut fungus

A FUNGUS DELICACY

One important parasitic species of fungus is the corn smut. On average, this smut destroys about two percent of corn crops. In addition to leaving corn with black, spore-filled kernels, the fungus also causes lumps to grow on the plant's stems, ears, or tassels. In Mexico, these lumps are eaten as a delicacy!

DANGEROUS SPORES

Parasitic club fungi live on animals, too. One particular species causes humans a problem. *Cryptococcus neoformans* normally grows on bird droppings and releases its spores into the air. People with weakened immune systems, including some people with AIDS, may become infected when they breathe in these spores. The disease that results is called cryptococcosis, and it can infect the lungs or the brain. It causes fever, fatigue, poor vision, and confusion. It can result in death.

Eater Beware: Poisonous Mushrooms

Each spring and fall, mushroom hunters head outdoors to find their favorite basidiocarps to eat. It takes some experience to be able to tell exactly which species are edible, which will give someone a stomachache, and which will kill.

One of the most deadly mushrooms is called the destroying angel. It is a flat, plate-like mushroom with white gills and a ring around the stalk. A single mushroom contains enough poison to kill a grown man, so avoiding all mushrooms with white gills is a good idea. Another poisonous species is bright orange, giving it the name Jack-o-lantern. Although eating this mushroom can cause mild to severe illness, it isn't life threatening. Many small brown mushrooms also contain poisons that will make a person ill. It is often difficult to tell the poisonous small brown species from the edible small brown ones, so it is best to avoid them all. It just isn't worth the risk!

HANDLE WITH CARE

Some mushrooms contain hallucinogenic substances and can be poisonous as well. One such mushroom, fly agaric (left), is known for its bright red or yellow cap and white spots. This colorful mushroom is poisonous, but most cautions surrounding its use have to do with its hallucinogenic properties and its ability to cause a person to experience false visions, smells, tastes, or sounds.

The white flesh of the highly poisonous destroying angel (right) has an unpleasant, sickly smell. Its taste is at first mild, then burning.

One Humongous Fungus

The thought of the largest organism in the world conjures up images of whales and elephants. In fact, the title goes to a fungus. The hyphae of this humongous individual grow underground over an area of nearly four square miles (10 square km)—enough land to hold as many as 1,600 football fields. Scientists discovered it in 2003, in the forests of Oregon. It is estimated to be between 2,000 and 10,000 years old and weighs in the same range as a blue whale. It belongs to the species *Armillaria ostoyae*, whose mushrooms commonly appear here and there in yellow brown clumps in woodlands each year. The discovery took the record of largest individual from another fungus one that lives on the Michigan-Wisconsin border. This individual *Armillaria bulbosa* covers 37 acres (15 hectares) and is also thought to be thousands of years old.

These humongous fungi have raised the question of what an "individual" might be. Each organism started from one spore and has identical DNA throughout, and so both are considered individuals. Or are they? What if at some time in the past, an organism broke into pieces, and each piece continued to grow separately. Can these parts still be called an individual?

These honey fungi are the fruiting bodies of the giant Armillaria ostoyae.

ARMILLARIA OSTOYAE	
Kingdom:	Fungi
Phylum:	Basidiomycota
Class:	Basidiomycetes
Order:	Agaricales
Family:	Marasmiaceae
Genus:	*Armillaria*
Species:	*Armillaria ostoyae*

Glossary

ascocarp The fruiting body of the Ascomycota, the sac fungi; morels and truffles are ascocarps

ascospores The spores produced by Ascomycota, the sac fungi, as a result of sexual reproduction

ascus The "spore factory" in Ascomycota, the sac fungi, that results from sexual reproduction; it always contains eight spores

asexual reproduction Reproduction in which an organism produces smaller copies of itself without combining with another individual

basidia The "spore factory" in Basidiomycota, the club fungi, that results from sexual reproduction; it is shaped like a club

basidiocarp The fruiting body of the Basidiomycota, the club fungi; mushrooms, toadstools, and puffballs are basidiocarps

basidiospores The spores produced by Basidiomycota, the club fungi, as a result of sexual reproduction

budding A means of asexual reproduction in which a unicellular organism produces a second nucleus and pushes the nucleus, along with other necessary cell parts, through its cell wall as a bud, which then breaks off to form a new organism

carnivore A meat eater

cell The smallest unit of life

classification The method scientists use to name and organize organisms into groups

conidiophore The "spore factory" of Ascomycota, the sac fungi, and Basidiomycota, the club fungi, that results from asexual reproduction

conidiospore The spores produced by mycelial Ascomycota and Basidiomycota, as a result of asexual reproduction

decompose To break down into smaller parts

DNA Deoxyribonucleic acid, a complex molecule that is the blueprint for life, which contains all the "instructions" for building cells; organisms reproduce by replicating their DNA

enzyme A protein in an organism that is key to making chemical reactions happen—for example, breaking down of food molecules in digestion

eukaryotic Having to do with organisms that have a nucleus and other cell parts separated from the rest of the cell by a membrane; plants, animals, fungi, and protists are eukaryotes

fruiting body The structure produced by fungi as a result of sexual reproduction that is the site of spore production and release

gene A segment of DNA that carries the information for a particular trait or the making of a particular protein

heterotrophs Organisms that obtain their nutrients (sugars and starches) from other organisms, dead or alive

hypha (plural *hyphae*) thin, thread-like structures consisting of fungal cells; most fungi exist and grow as hyphae

immune system An animal's defenses against parasites and disease

metabolism The use of energy; the processes that occur within an organism to sustain life

mold Fuzzy growth of a fungus on dead or alive tissue of an organism

molecule A grouping of two or more atoms bonded together; the smallest unit of a chemical compound that can take part in a chemical reaction

mutualist An organism—or having to do with organisms—living in a symbiotic association that benefits both organisms

mycelium (plural *mycelia*) The collective mass of hyphae of a growing fungus

nucleus (plural *nuclei*) The part of the cell where DNA is located

nutrients Molecules used by the body for growth, repair, and reproduction

organism A living being; can refer to an individual or a species

photosynthesis The chemical process by which energy from sunlight is used to make carbohydrates (sugars) using carbon dioxide and water

primitive Relating to an early stage in the development of an organism

prokaryote A unicellular organism whose cells do not have a nucleus or other cell parts that are separated from the rest of the cell by a membrane; bacteria and archaea are prokaryotes

reproduce To replicate

saprotrophic Having to do with organisms that obtain their carbohydrate nutrients (sugars and starches) from dead organisms; saprotrophs decompose organisms

septum (plural *septa*) Cross walls that divide the cells of fungi; they are regularly spaced in the hyphae of sac fungi and club fungi

sexual reproduction Reproduction in which an organism joins with another individual of the same species and exchanges DNA; the new organisms that are produced contain DNA from both individuals

species A group of individual organisms that have enough of a similar genetic makeup that they are able to mate and exchange DNA

spore A tiny unit, often consisting of one cell, that is capable of giving rise to a new individual organism

symbiotic Having to do with the association of two organisms living close to one another, usually resulting in benefits to one or both of the organisms

termite A small, soft-bodied insect that lives in large, well-organized colonies, usually within nests or mounds of compacted soil; termites feed off of dead plants, including wood, and can do extensive damage to buildings and other structures

toxin A poison or venom introduced to an organism, usually from a plant or an animal, usually resulting in disease

vitamins Nutrients required in small quantities that are not used as building blocks but rather are involved in chemical reactions

zygospores The spores produced by Zygomycota, the pin molds, as a result of asexual reproduction

Further Information

www.doctorfungus.org
Everything you ever wanted to know about fungi that cause disease, and then some. People, plants, animals, and even buildings are discussed.

www.uoguelph.ca/~gbarron
Professor George Barron writes articles about some of the most interesting fungi in the world. He includes a lot of great photos in his articles, too. There's a special section of articles called "War of the Worlds: Fungi vs. the Rest."

www.exploratorium.edu/cooking/bread/bread_science.html
This Web site shows how yeast works to make bread and offers a yeasty experiment to do at home.

www.botany.hawaii.edu/faculty/wong/BOT135/Lect16.htm
This Web site discusses how fungi are used to make foods, including bread, cheese, soy sauce, and tempeh.

tomvolkfungi.net
Professor Tom Volk loves fungi—and it shows. This site has tons of information about fungi and features a new species every month.

herbarium.usu.edu/fungi/FunFacts/factindx.htm
The title of this Web site says it all: *Fun Facts about Fungus.* In addition to fascinating fact sheets, there are games and experiments to try here.

www.wildmanstevebrill.com
Wildman Steve Brill eats wild mushrooms as well as other plants. This fun Web site has great photos and simple descriptions.

www.ac.wwu.edu/~fredr/3D_Photo_Main.htm
Three-dimensional fungi photographs. They're beautiful and diverse, but there's a trick to viewing them in 3-D!

www.backyardnature.net/f/2fungi.htm
What fungi live in your backyard? This Web site will point you to places to look. There are a lot of disease-causing fungi, decomposers, and mycorrhiza to find.

Index

Index

ABOUT THE AUTHOR

Judy Wearing has been writing about science for more than ten years. She has a Ph.D. in biology from the University of Oxford and is a qualified educator. Her most recent book is *Edison's Concrete Piano* (ECW Press, 2009). When not writing, Judy can be found on her hobby farm milking the goat or walking the dogs.